THE BUSY SATURDAY WORD BOOK

by Bruce Isen / *illustrated by* Ellen Dolce

A GOLDEN BOOK • NEW YORK

Western Publishing Company, Inc., Racine, Wisconsin 53404

Copyright © 1985 by Western Publishing Company, Inc. Illustrations copyright © 1985 by Ellen Dolce. All rights reserved. Printed in the U.S.A. No part of this book may be reproduced or copied in any form without written permission from the publisher. GOLDEN®, GOLDEN & DESIGN®, A GOLDEN TELL-A-TALE® BOOK, and A GOLDEN BOOK® are trademarks of Western Publishing Company, Inc. Library of Congress Catalog Card Number: 85-70335. ISBN 0-307-07003-4   C D E F G H I J

window shade

clock

pillow

comforter

toy chest

blocks

night
light

bed

top

dresser

It's Saturday morning. Angie wakes up early
and plays till breakfast time.

spoons

kettle

stove

toaster

oven

milk

eggs

whisk

flour

waffle iron

"Let's have a special breakfast," Daddy says.

juicer

oranges

butter

"What do you want to do this morning?"
Mommy asks.
"Let's go to the park!" Angie cries.
So they do.

monkey bars

kite

seesaw

swing

sifter

pail

shovel

ball

sandbox

rooster

hutch

rabbits

turnstile

kid

chicks

ducks

shed

pony

Then they walk across the park to the
children's zoo.

"Now we have errands to do," Mommy says.
"Let's take a walk in town."

Mommy goes to the drugstore.

drills

rope

wrenches

saws

screwdrivers

hammers

gloves

pliers

Daddy and Angie go to the hardware store.

Then they all go to Trimbles department store. Angie needs a new jacket.

blouses

mirror

jacket

skirts

dresses

"Are you hungry, Angie?" Daddy asks.
"I sure am," Angie says.
They go to the diner for lunch.

jukebox

coat
rack

menu

booth

blender

freezer

counter

pies

cake
stand

stool

phonograph

records

bookcase

table

chair

After lunch, they go to the library. Angie returns the books she has read. Then she chooses some others she hasn't read.

"What do you want to do for the rest of the afternoon?" Daddy asks.

"Let's go to the movie!" Angie says.

"Good idea," says Daddy.

The movie is about people in outer space.

stars

alien

popcorn

aisle

EXIT

flag

planet

spacecraft

screen

astronauts

curtain

tunnel

track

locomotive

caboose

station

After the movie, they go home. Angie and Daddy play till supper is ready.

Before they eat, the family says grace.

faucets

washcloth

soap

tub

duckie

bath mat

towels

hamper

toilet

sink

Later, Angie takes a bath.

After her busy day, Angie is ready for bed.
First Daddy reads her a story.

vase

painting

lamp

armchair

fireplace

rug

robe

banister

teddy
bear

pajamas

staircase

Then she goes upstairs.
Good night!